Wells

D1714073

Wells

JENNA BUTLER

THE UNIVERSITY OF ALBERTA PRESS

Published by
The University of Alberta Press
Ring House 2
Edmonton, Alberta, Canada T6G 2E1
www.uap.ualberta.ca

Copyright © 2012 Jenna Butler

LIBRARY AND ARCHIVES CANADA CATALOGUING IN PUBLICATION

Butler, Jenna, 1980–
     Wells / Jenna Butler.

(Robert Kroetsch series of Canadian creative works)
Poems.
ISBN 978-0-88864-606-4

     I. Title. II. Series: Robert Kroetsch series of Canadian creative works

PS8603.U84W45 2012   C811'.6   C2012-900155-4

First edition, first printing, 2012.
Printed and bound in Canada by Houghton Boston Printers, Saskatoon, Saskatchewan.
Copyediting and proofreading by Peter Midgley.

A volume in the Robert Kroetsch series.

The University of Alberta Press is committed to protecting our natural environment. As part of our efforts, this book is printed on Enviro Paper: it contains 100% post-consumer recycled fibres and is acid- and chlorine-free.

The University of Alberta Press gratefully acknowledges the support received for its publishing program from The Canada Council for the Arts. The University of Alberta Press also gratefully acknowledges the financial support of the Government of Canada through the Canada Book Fund (CBF) and the Government of Alberta through the Alberta Multimedia Development Fund (AMDF) for its publishing activities.

In memory of my grandmother,
Muriel Rosalie Ellen Butler

Anchorage

In Julian's alone unlettered hand
love takes the hard ground

dust of oak-
gall and the quill, the history of the soul. It breaks

an April into tiny unprotected revelations
of its own. It makes bone

flower like blackthorn.

—GILLIAN ALLNUTT

Contents

Wells

1

The north sea speaks carefully around a mouthful of flints.

The beach is a buzzard feast, salted carnage. Miles upon miles of razor clams, caught by the headland, butterfly open under a cacophony of gulls. This is not the image you had held of this place, but it is right, if ironic. Memory has pinioned this beach as a place of calm; a dimly-recalled mother in housedress and cardigan, pockets bulging with hoarded stones, walking through the surf. At home, a telegram she had not allowed you to see, detailing the loss of your older brother at Normandy. Sitting on the beach in wellies and bathing suit, you wondered if she might not walk out into the sea. She was already weighted down with stones; it wouldn't have been much of a stretch. And she might have done, with greater impact. As it is, you have no recollection of her disappearance from memory. Her image simply filmed over like a dimming eye; sank cleanly and without fuss.

Out from the shelter of the pine woods, the wind along the tide line scours the lungs with unceremonious brutality. Sandwiches and tabbouleh in the beach bag over your shoulder, the smell of mint leaking from the Tupperware. On an ideal day, you'd slip out of your sandals and test the water with false bravado, feet so slim and pale they hurt to look at. Today, though, doing so would be risking excoriation; clams pock the sand like chipped teeth, fragments from a war you knew nothing about.

You curl into the sand, your hands folded in front of your face. The veins stand haphazard and blue, scuttling crazed like Hadrian's Wall. Around us, the wind dips and chews; the dunes shift in protest.

Into the holes in your mind, I trail breadcrumbs, poke words like tongue in a smile gone gaptoothed. The paucity of what's solid. The overgenerous space. *Tern. Tideline.* Watch you hold for a moment, your face twisted with naming, then slide slack. This, the way of doldrums: sudden, that theft, all forward momentum gone.

I watch you watching terns, lips groping after language.

Becalmed.

3

There was an aunt in Battersea who never came out of the war.
How easy it was then to lose one woman amidst a whole country
dredging itself from the Blitz. Everyone walking wounded. It
was not her body but her words that failed, however, petering
themselves out in the new Covent Garden Market over parsnips,
Darjeeling, Ceylon. She found herself deconstructed word by
word until housebound, where only muscle memory told her
how to poach fish, and that she did, after all, take sugar with tea.
In the back garden, the old Doyenne pear blossomed frantically,
its crown alight with bees. She watched as the fruits came,
blushing, thrusting their rotund bodies against the window glass.
Their scent was peremptory, drifting throughout the house.

You visited her only once before the Home, before the stroke
that left body and mind wracked and gone. Early summer, the
house rank with the scent of overripe fruit. A stilted lunch in
the living room, the plaster peeling from age and damp, and
how she ate pears with the tears running down her face.

You knew that the words were leaving you when your back was turned. They were getting out somehow—subterfuge, disguise, swimming the moat. Bedsheets strung together like semaphore flags from an outside wall. The tricky part was catching them in the act. Bemused rather than angry, you'd ask, *How can you miss something when you don't even realize it's gone? When you don't even remember its presence in the first place?*

We unearthed your notes in arcane places. *Take off parking brake*, in a careful hand. *Mozzarella, not good for fondue.* And once, on the bird table in faded Biro, *Greenfinches prefer peanuts.*

When you could no longer remember that you kept a package of Post-Its in your shirt pocket, the notes appeared in whatever was to hand. The house became a litany of your absences. Indelible marker on the dryer, cribbed careful and small. *Bleach only with whites.* On the medicine cabinet in the bathroom, once in desperation: *Sleeping pills. TWO only.*

As if it'd make any difference. As if you'd wake up one day and your mind would pick itself up again, put together all those myriad fragments. The Post-Its, tidily recording every bit as it slipped. The markers, the Biros, the pencil jottings on Formica under the placemat on your side of the table. The list in thin black felt-tip on your wrist, kissing up to your skin like some bizarre tattoo. The words for half a dozen different vegetables. Under the cuff, faintly, and where you thought I might not see, my name.

One day, there will be more of those notes than you will have words. One day, I will gather them together and reassemble you.

5

That? *Tern. It skips over the waves, airstrike, its cry angling behind it.* Those plants. *Sea lavender, that purple haze over the saltings. Samphire. Glasswort.* Pine trees? *Corsican. Holm oaks behind.* What's this? *The fork? Or do you mean*—No, this. *Tabbouleh. Bulgur and tomato. Parsley. Lemon. Mint.* (A slow smile, eyes brightening, hanging on.) Mint, yes, from the garden. It got its roots in there and it never came out. Yards of the stuff.

It got its roots in there and it never came out.

All the names I know, and the only one I don't want to:

this.

You used to be able to talk around the gaps, find words that were right enough, with acrobatic deftness. Now your tongue trips, mind falls flat like marram grass in a sea gale. Your leaps of logic confound even you, leave your listeners coughing into their hands, frantic for distraction.

You loved this beach once. The wind, the way it rips off the sea on a blustery day, what it drives up onto the sand. Whelks, polished stones, gull feathers battered like spindles. Bottle glass, bright colours scarified, filmed over. The same look in your eyes now when you turn to me, unsure, not wanting to ask.

Flight

1

Sometimes I get through the day solely because there are birds.

Spring months, sky clocking almost blue. Over the salt marshes, a linnet in aerobatic flight, its song pealing like rain. Transitory as the moon, whimbrels on stilt legs, their fluted bills and panpipe call.

April, and you have left me in every way but flesh. There are grasshopper warblers nesting in the old flint quarry, their namesake silver thrum flashing from the bracken. Sound of neurons misfiring; beyond language, the tone of the body leaving itself. Ventriloquial. *Wherever you are, be somewhere else.*

3

I have taken to walking in the mornings beyond sight of the sea, its endless heave of loss.

The lane back of the sea road holds a different cast of characters, the regulars you loved best. Meadow pipits stalking spiders, buffeting each other upward in a mad, startled rush. In the hedgerows, coal tits, wheatears. Dunnocks shuffling like old men in the brambles.

Near the common one summer, we stopped to watch cattle on the green. On the fence, two robins dashing a riposte at a startled jackdaw. The smallest things made you chuckle, then; those robins, persimmon, indignant.

4

This brittle clock skitters into fall, sheaves piled and suddenly,
one morning, dotted with bramblings, fieldfares. Two evenings
into October, I stop for a herd on the coast road and a nightjar's
call churrs through the car window. Such a strange sound, dry-twig
rattle. That knuckled clatter, the season turning over.

5

Winter comes early, brings a skiff of snow. Settles its long shankbones across the saltings.

For days, few birds dare the windy stretch of beach. I turn the collar of your houndstooth jacket, already willing to trade gale winds for summer's purl of tide.

In the garden, frost binds the firecrest voiceless, the treecreepers knotted along branches, clicking their darning bills. At dusk, the barn owls drift soundless, grey and peat against the dark. They have stitched themselves along the rafters of the old hay barn near the common. At my entrance, the collective ruffle of feathers like indrawn breath. The flash of countless eyes before exhale, and flight.

6

The house empties with your presence, sound bleeding out at the edges. A mistle thrush calls from the coal shed roof, and I see your eyes flare briefly before the inevitable blank.

You saw a storm petrel, you told me once, out along the coast road. Nothing else it could be, you enthused, its feet skittering on the water as it dipped low to feed. The delight of it banked against my disbelief, your complete faith in that small, black-glossed bird.

Couldn't have been, I wanted to say. *They only come in gale-tossed, and rarely off the North Sea. They make landfall to mate, and then only at night, on the turning breeze.*

You don't see them coming, but you can hear them. A great, rolling susurrus, like the evening given voice. And in behind it, the sound of loss. Silence precipitating tangibly.

The same sound leaking from this house, night-dip of a black wing.

Garden

1

Your father, cheerful in worsted and Donegal tweed, spade cocked over one shoulder, taught you all he knew of earth.

Larkspur, he named, its ultraviolet bells agog with bees. Love-in-a-mist, punch of blue in a jacksnipe of prickles.

3

His favourite was none of these. At the bottom of the garden, half hidden amongst the nettles, rose rhubarb-like plumes of green flowers. Mignonette, he named them, tapping the stems with a stick. The scent, piercingly sweet and sudden, threatened to break open the world.

Midsummer, when the cistern ran dry, your father walked to the
quarry with a yoke of buckets. Back and forth he went, up and down
the lane, bringing the cool, sweet quarry water spangled with lime.
The walk itself becoming meditation, like his slow, calm way of
greeting each plant by name.

5

When you came upon your father in the tool shed, he was invariably tending to his spade with a file and a bucket of oiled sand. Ashwood and smithy-forged iron an extension of his arm, the dull thunk of blade slicing into daylily roots. You had long been attuned to this tool, its twin actions of building and division. Its scarred black head nodding over your father's shoulder, off to coax a new bed from the flinty soil.

After rain, how he scythed it down to crush the anemone snouts of moles as they came up for air.

6

Naming is taken like this, sudden arc of iron.

Day's eye, your father would say—a flower in love with the passing sun.

Your face, jaundiced and irresolute, couched in an aureole of white hair. A rare calm moment, eyes turned to the window. Clocking the light.

Home

1

Home was only a word, a small box bursting at the edges with an idea too big to be contained. What spoke to you of home in this place once were the scents. The narcissus in brilliant, fragrant drifts outside the kitchen window, strung along the foot of the yew hedge like fairy lights. The rose garden you planted outside the coal shed after the War, as though with every blossom's emergence, you could force the depravity of those years outside the bounds of memory.

2

The coal shed's scent was a memory apart. Black and metallic, somehow smelling of death, although no blood was involved. The copper-rust tang of the scuttle, the clouds of coal dust billowing, acrid and faintly venomous.

As a child, twice a day you'd be sent to the shed, bearing the empty scuttle before you in a gesture reminiscent of warding. The key was to nip in the breath and fill the scuttle as quickly as you could. Burst out of the shed and into the rain-washed air, gasping and pink-cheeked. You'd heard the adults talk about coal dust. Fathers of friends were miners, rough, winter-pale men with battered hands and deep, hacking coughs. You imagined the dust coalescing inside their lungs, its dark smell of iron and black water. Filling those men until it displaced them entirely.

3

The kitchen smelt often of quince. The hoary fruits inedible unless cooked, whereupon they resolved into a spring-pink jelly.

Inevitably, all other scents would be underwritten by tea. The Darjeeling your mother was so fond of, your father's chicory coffee, a taste he'd developed during the War. How your mother tried to break him of it, that coffee, its scent bitter and deeply medicinal. He'd tell her, *Habits aren't horseshoes; they can't be thrown so easily.*

He came back from the War overwritten with translucent patches, the scar tissue gleaming as though he'd been drizzled with molten glass. Wherever the mustard gas had touched, it had burned, clear through the wool tunic and out along his limbs like marsh fire. When the sunlight found him now, it did so gingerly, his skin coming alight in silver, the scars blazing. As though, in stripping everything away from him, the gas had somehow given him this armour. He no longer rolled up his sleeves in the garden as he hefted the spade, worried that someone might be moved to pity. Your father came back from the War armoured inside his own skin. Against everything.

Even his own family.

Even you.

Spring brought out the hawthorn along the Common Road, brilliant white and musky. Before the rain, that scent was almost animal in its intensity, tiny blossoms flinging themselves bright and blind against the sky. Only a good storm could stroke the desperation out of those flowers. They became contrite then, as though they had thoroughly blasted themselves on that one fever pitch of scent. They would hold defiantly to their branches for a day or so afterward, and when they fell at last, the old Shire horse would be brought out from Spring Hill and the rickety old wagon would carry the workers down to the fields to sow out the wheat.

The hawthorn's scent vanished overnight. The old mare, Seldom Swift, plodded along in harness, and in the wake of her wagon came the green rush of summer.

5

You were thirty, heavy with twins. When the bicycle upended on the asphalt road, you lost the scent of the coal shed, your mother's tea. The roses in the sideyard garden.

Your face healed within weeks, but when your boys were born, part of them was gone from you. They were beautiful children, bright-haired. You watched your daughter drawing the babies to her face, inhaling their sweet milk scent.

It was only years later, when she had a child of her own and realized that you could not even smell the bread burning in the oven, that your daughter understood the extent of what you had lost.

6

The narcissus are nodding again outside the kitchen window, faint breath of winter's leaving fingering their stems.

In your mind, the scent of the blossoms evàdes your reach. Like so much else now, there is simply an echo where that sweetness should be. The aftershock that follows the tolling of a bell.

Behind your eyes, your father stands, turns away. The momentary flash of his scars catching the light.

Grain

1

Stay out of the barley during August, they warned, *when the stalks grow tight and tall and you cannot see the ground.*

2

Should have known better. Should have known that forbidding is as good as daring to children who have lived all their lives within sight of barley fields. Children who have lain on their backs under dryhusk curtains of golden heads, sky tessellated with barley beards. Under their skin, June-gold light, echoes of men working the thresher crews up in the high field. Between their teeth, bitter, hard grains, somehow more real than any summer fruit.

3

To dare the barley fields with your brother was an act of faith. The scant half-mile of swaying grain turned limber gauntlet for three weeks every year when the hornets nested. Nothing saved you from those lividly buzzing fields; not wellingtons to the knee, not the mad, frenzied dash affected at each humming cataclysm. Walking became blind faith. Hornets had been known to pursue fieldworkers all the way back to the village. *Tarantella*, the dance of the spider-bitten, passionate and brief, dervish-bright. The dance that rode the fieldworkers bore no name, their spastic marionette limbs thrashing. Bodies caught in perpetual jag; wanting to brush off the thrum, wanting to flee.

4

He caught your uncle drowning barn kittens in the quarry pond. An anonymous burlap seed sack, a couple of broken bricks. Realizing he was watched, your uncle made no move to retrieve the sack from the water. Your brother lit out through the grain. No more than seven, the sinuous barley whipcracking back behind him, slithering into place. It took your uncle's men half an hour to find him, leaving, as he did, no trail.

5

When at last they came near, the ground itself was heaving with hornets. They had swarmed your brother when he fell, his face a limpid golden mask. Took weeks for the men's stings to abate, for your brother's body to reform itself out of a mass of swelling.

6

All through the autumn, his voice rasped from the hornets' poison, battered windpipe slow to heal. He wheezed deep in his chest, his voice skittering like something small and angry and winged.

He

smelt of pipesmoke and peat, sour waft of whiskey sweat, rich scent of earth. Out hunting with the fieldworkers, he was sent downwind where the rabbits could not get the breeze off him, his jacket redolent of Black Cut Cavendish.

Your mother hounded him for it, but he was never without that pipe, tight-grained cherry burl, tamped down hard and scarcely gleaming. His lapels shingled with ash.

Twice, he flushed a kettle of hawks from the scrub on a turning wind. A sudden, vagrant breeze; the grass underfoot exploding into flight.

lost his brother, your uncle, who died and was laid out in the parlour, the room instantaneously settling into factions. Women in the kitchen, fretting over food: was there enough, what to do with duplicates, did anyone serve jellied ham at a wake. The men gathered in the parlour, encircling the coffin, passing a tin of tobacco.

The incongruity of it; opening the door like lifting a veil. The men's faces recalled dimly out of the haze, summoned to dinner, and every last one of them smelling of your father. The Cavendish, and under that, after the tin had run out, Bright Virginia.

The dead man, your uncle, abandoned in the fuggy parlour. When you bent to place a kiss on his cheek, he, too, smelt of your father. Or your father of him. Black Cut. Swift death in a late summer field. Your uncle, your father; the way death spun down suddenly on these men, catching them out, waiting for them beyond calling distance.

3

took up tobacco on the approach to Arnhem in '44.

They would shoot for the light of your cigarette, he'd say, *the German snipers. One man next to me, he lit up, and bang. Just like that. Straight through the eye.*

You could tamp your pipe tight and smoke it downward so that they couldn't see. And it kept the rain out...that interminable rain.

smelt of something other than smoke on one lone day in the week.
Sundays, and him in his church best. Trousers with creases and
overstarched shirts. *Something your mother does to keep me from falling asleep
during the service.* Told wryly, him standing at the back door, looking
out over his garden. Large hands curiously, unseemingly idle. This
day, its particular restraint, needling him when there was work to
be done in the vegetable plot. Weeds didn't stop for the Sabbath.

What he gave up for her, your mother. Among other things, this day,
this weekly doldrum. His thumb circling the pipe bowl in his vest
pocket, his strangely absent scent, as though some essential part of
him had been momentarily cut away.

Standing at the door, stunned by inaction, by love. Smelling of
nothing. Just the rain.

5

would sit with your uncle on autumn evenings before he died. The day coming down early outside, faltering on into winter.

Indoors, smoke and whiskey, men's voices rumbling, fire-dazzle through cut-glass tumblers. Never enough to stagger them, but enough to turn the season. A send-off of sorts, the harvest safely in, winter wheat drilled and the fields standing momentarily empty of anything but light.

If your mother joined them, she took sherry, but you secretly believed she must have hankered after that whiskey. How could she not. The burr smell of it, the one contraband nip he allowed you.

You imagined it lighting him, body gone glass, a spirit lamp burning. Proof, somehow, against the dark.

lost his scent the morning he died.

It came to pieces in your hands, watching the undertaker's discreet
car slip away from the door. Knowing the gap he left in that house;
the way your mother's earlier absence had resounded for him,
clapping the rooms like a startled bell.

He was tidied into a new suit, one he wore only for best, that didn't
smell like him. Like anything. He gleamed in the coffin. Hair lacquer,
cologne. All traces of the garden eased from under his fingernails.

The house as shiftless as you. Robbed in a way not yet understood.

His tweed gardening coat from the hall cupboard; how you wore it in
your own garden until the elbows rubbed out. His scent breathed out
of the collar, inhaled to vanishing.

& She

1

had a tongue like a whipcrack, upstart Catherine wheel. She was the only woman you ever knew who could make tone into epithet; after the Wars, the only one who could reach into your father and jerk him back out of himself. Clack of internal monologue cracking its spine. His eyes interrupted, verdigris with fury.

Grateful.

had gotten to the sixth year at the limewashed village school. In spite of this, she was canny, bright in a way that made other women's eyes click away when they met her own. They said she sewed fair, had a shrewish tongue and too much the measure of her husband. By birth, she was one of them. By nature, she discomfited. Lilacs on her table, the house funereal with their scent.

3

moved the farthest she'd ever gone in her life when she married your father and shifted one parish over. Her old home within walking distance; might as well have been miles once she took his name. It was as easy as that in those days, the liminal space between girl and woman. You let down your hemline and you put up your hair. If you were lucky, your old churchyard was close enough that you could put flowers on the family graves one Sunday a month.

That's what marrying meant for her. She lost her freedom and she kept her dead.

soon learned that this is what happens when a house turns against
a woman.

An oak comes down on the slate roof and cracks snake across
the ceilings, malignant, with a tendency to shift overnight. Every
windblown ash seed finds its roots in the eavestroughing; the garden
goes to stinging nettle and mint. What breaks in the cupboard:
uncertain, but the black ichor lingers for days.

Pantry inventory: three bottles of homemade wine.

Vinegar, vinegar, burst.

Gypsies in the front garden, vardo blocking the Common Road and
shifting like a wide-rigged schooner. Eager dark eyes at the kitchen
window.

What they expected, it wasn't you.

5

knew only one thing for certain: honour the dead.

Lambing time. Such white bundles, the cords looped and pulled blue.

Lone thatcher flayed on ridgeline, his son gone spread-eagled against sky.

Snowdrops in the burying ground.

A shattered sparrow, feet curling like leaves.

long outlived him, your father. His skin so scarred that no matter which way you turned him, he caught the light.

And now you, making your way through her kitchen, years of living in this house that never wanted her. Bone china teacups (mismatched wedding sets), handleless. How she'd knocked them off against the stovetop in a fit of pique when her joints swelled, knuckles catching in the handles' hoops.

Straightforward, people called her. Canny. And yet, this: under the kitchen sink, a wicker basket of oak clothes pegs caught at the tops with rings of brass. Gypsy pins, she called them. *Always buy something from a gypsy*, she'd tell you, *or they'll curse your home.*

At one corner of her gate, visible only under scrutiny, was a faint chalk line. A gypsy mark. *This is a good house; you'll be welcome here.*

The irony of it. A line of chalk, a handful of gypsy pins. And in the end, she was the one unwelcome in her own house.

Flesh

1

Corset.

Crinoline.

Petticoat.

Girdle.

Stockings. (Silk, if you saved for them. Nylon, during the War.)

Buttons. (In their hundreds, hard enough to bruise fingertips, appetites. Pearl.)

Layers upon layers that had you gasping, fanning. Summers a horror, nothing so cool as picture houses, dance halls, caverns where young people pressed hot bodies in the fan-loud darkness.

In the country, only sticky heat. The village too tiny to warrant even a café and soda fountain, though during the second War, the council pulled up all the road signs anyway. Stop the Germans from finding the village on foot.

Nonsense was your London father getting lost on the back roads coming in from work, the signposts gone and him sweating through his jacket all the six miles home.

3

In spite of it all, there were pregnancies. Seemingly impenetrable costumes proved fallible, in spite of outfits designed to keep a man's hands off a girl. A girl's hands off herself. Everything battened down like storm doors...suddenly sprung in a late-night hayfield.

The boys going off to war. The girls teetering on the edge of stasis. A furnace summer, barley beards clattering around the grains like reliquaries.

Growing up, you were touched by so many things.

Schubert and rain, the liquid feel of new gloves. Dog rose, hawthorn, sour green sloes just beginning to purple. The taste of them astringent on your tongue.

At the edge of the hayfield, a flag of corn poppies, sunset lifting their skirts like a Guy Fawkes fire.

The hands of your husband and those of your children.

You were touched by so many things.

5

As you began to disappear, you wanted to hold my hand. Of your remaining words, *anchor* was the one you found.

You couldn't always recall my name, but you knew my touch. A palm on your shoulder, five fingers curling against collarbone, and you'd unfold as though whatever had crumpled you had suddenly drawn your strings straight.

You craved tastes, colours, half-remembered things you couldn't name. I brought you oranges, peppermints. A bright scarf of crepe silk that caught at our fingertips.

Finer and finer the things that hold us. Until one day, whatever keeps you here slips. Anchorless, your silver head bobbing toward sleep. My hand on your shoulder, your blue eyes vacant as sea, as sky.

6

Your chair has been wheeled out into the garden so you can sit in the sun.

What birds there are this time of year are singing, and perhaps it registers. The sun touches you with a warmth you cannot remember, cannot name. It slip-slides along your skin at the edge of consciousness.

Beyond worry, there is a space you inhabit like a shell. Its small calm, the way light falls through and illuminates, passes on.

Grief, like memory, tasked to those of us left behind.

The late afternoon sun slanting down. This body going on without you.

Nothing is intelligible without the past,
not because it is the past, but because it is the missing body of the present.

    —ADAM NICOLSON

Author's Notes

This is not my story.

It is not hers alone, either; my grandmother.

It is a tale that shifts so many of us, nudges us from our axes. After a loved one vanishes into Alzheimer's or dementia, we are tilted off true somehow. It is not just the loss of the ones we care for, but the loss of ourselves in them, seeing our own lives erased from memory until we are left doubting, in a deep place, the truth of our own existence.

Memory is like this, a tentative weft. One story unpicked and the whole threatens to unravel.

This collection is, then, an homage to all the things that underpin memory. Stories: some of them true, some overheard, extrapolated, or fabricated. Scents, images, places imaginary and real. Everything tatted together.

These words are all I have to give to the grandmother I so deeply love, who, for years, has not known my face, let alone my name.

Acknowledgements

For D&S, and stories shared

For C&Y, and that day at Wells

For T, memory-keeper, *mit Liebe*

The title of this collection comes from the town of Wells-next-the-Sea, England.

Many thanks to *Room* magazine for providing a home for the title poem "Wells," and to the 2009 Edmonton Poetry Festival / 2009 League of Canadian Poets Western Swing Tour for giving "Wells" its first major public performance.

Thanks to Peter Midgley, Cathie Crooks, and everyone at the University of Alberta Press for their generous time and support in bringing this book to life, and to Jonathan Meakin for having faith in this collection from the start.

I am indebted to the following authors for their quotations in this book:

Gillian Allnutt, *How the Bicycle Shone: New & Selected Poems* (Bloodaxe Books, 2007).

Denise Riley, *Mop Mop Georgette: New and Selected Poems 1986–1993* (Reality Street Editions, 1996). The title of her poem "Wherever you are, be somewhere else" is represented as a line in the poem "Flight."

Finally, grateful appreciation to the Alberta Foundation for the Arts for its generous support during the writing of this book.

OTHER TITLES FROM THE UNIVERSITY OF ALBERTA PRESS

Memory's Daughter

ALICE MAJOR

144 pages | cuRRents, a Canadian literature series
978–0–88864–539–5 | $24.95 (T) paper
Poetry/Canadian Literature

Too Bad

Sketches Toward a Self-Portrait

ROBERT KROETSCH

112 pages | cuRRents, a Canadian literature series
978–0–88864–537–1 | $24.95 (T) paper
Poetry/Canadian Literature

Kat Among the Tigers

KATH MACLEAN

96 pages | cuRRents, a Canadian literature series
978–0–88864–552–4 | $19.95 (T) paper
Poetry/Canadian Literature